The Joy
Of
No Self

- Reflections on the Nondual nature of everything.

By
Mandi Solk

All photos and poems in this book are by Mandi Solk

ISBN 978-0-9559819-0-6

This book wrote itself.

The words come directly from 'Presence'

and that which is reading this book

right now, is the same Presence.

When reading these pages, the *aliveness* may be found in-between the words and lines. As Debussy said: "Music is the silence between the notes". (He also said: "In opera there is too much singing!)

Being

No trace of Truth in a human face
Only the Love that fills all space
No 'me' over here
No 'you' over there
No person who can 'be aware'
Liberation is here right now
No-*one* can possibly teach you how

To the restless mind this will never be clear
It's beyond the reach of mortal ear
Being is found in the still, quiet space
Bearing witness of itself in every place
Yet there's nowhere that It can*not* be found
It's both the silence and the sound.

It has many names, like 'God' or 'Being'
Talked about in 'glimpses' and 'seeing'
But all the while there's no-thing to 'see'
It's simply found where there's no-*one* to BE

Preface

There are a host of different adjectives used to describe the indescribable: 'This' - 'It' - 'Being' - 'Spaciousness' - 'Energy' - 'God' etc. and these are just the English words – there are many more names used in other countries, especially in India. In Christian Science, there are seven synonyms for God: *Life; Love; Truth; Spirit; Soul; Mind; Principal* . Also, the name 'God' translates as the word 'Good' in many other languages. However, I often use the term: "I am' - meaning the 'I am presence', the only possible 'I' – which is and encompasses all.' Sometimes I simply call it 'Love'.

Some communicators of Non-Duality may avoid using the words: 'Love' and 'God' because of the religious or romantic connotations; but the true nature of Love is beyond any classification or boundary that the human mind could apply.

Love is All in All and therefore it is absolutely non-dualistic because it fills all space and *is* also the space that it fills. No-one can ever be outside of Love because they are also composed of it. There is no separation – Love is all in all.

If you were to ask a Quantum Physicist about the nature of the world, they would probably tell you that everything is energy – and many of them have no satisfactory words to describe

11

that energy other than God. Everything and everyone is made of the same 'stuff' – we are literally *spiritual* in substance. 'Love' is substance. This is what is meant in the Bible when we are described as being the 'image and likeness of God'. We are all God and there is nothing outside of God. There are no people there is only God, Love, bearing witness of itself.

Imagine a huge diamond, stretching from floor to ceiling displaying thousands of brilliant multi-coloured facets. The various colours of the facets reflected appear real. For instance, a deep blue facet may look solidly blue, but on closer inspection, it's found just to be transparent and clear. All the various glinting facets of the diamond may seem like true colours, but in fact there are no individual colours – it's all just the one colourless diamond.

This describes the truth about 'people' – there aren't any real people. Each 'person' simply reflects another facet of the whole. Up close and truly seen, there is no-one there – nobody home – just an appearance of body & personality, as in the illusion of colour in the diamond – inhabited by no-one. Transparent and empty.

Mandi's Herstory

As there is no 'time', no past or future, then what I am about to relate is really just a story of an apparent past belonging to nobody. There is no further interest, belief or attachment to it. The story is a complete dream of a 'past' that I am describing *now*. Memories are just thoughts arising *presently* in consciousness, therefore they have no relevance. But it's fun to write!

I was brought up in a middle-class family with 2 parents, an older brother and sister and a dog. I was given every material thing I ever wanted, but I was mystified with the world and deeply unhappy and sad, with a huge feeling of lack from about as far back as I can remember. This was no-one's fault and much of the time I might've appeared to everyone that I was perfectly happy, but the truth was very different.

I had terrifying nightmares most nights, and in the days I felt lonely and very needy of love and approval. I'm sure I was a real problem to my family and so different from them. They've occasionally referred to me as the 'alien!'

However, we all get along fine now, but growing up was bewildering and distressing for me, and I truly felt lost and utterly alone. It was an ordeal.

In my private moments, I was always seeking another world – another reality other than the one I was in. In my 'other' world everything was mystical, magical, and innocent, and all the inhabitants were very kind, (and never shouted). I was always talking to 'God' and *looking* for God. I felt that the 'real' world was very hostile and I always seemed to be getting into trouble both at home and at school. Teachers and kids bullied me a lot in all the schools I went to, but most of the time I kept this quiet and told nobody, for fear of being told that I was being 'too dramatic!'.

I left home when I was eighteen and followed every spiritual and religious path I could find. I also studied everything psychic and 'supernatural' – looking for another world where I may find peace and a sense of 'home'. I soon got a real glimpse of this through the following experience:

I was riding down a busy high street on my motor-bike when I suddenly noticed a woman get into her car and drive straight out of her parking space and into the middle of the road without looking anywhere at all! Not even out of her window or rear-view mirror.

I slowed right down, but it was no use. I thought: "I'm going to die – there's nothing I can do – she's just keeping on going, without looking anywhere, and I can't do anything about it now, except aim to land on my helmeted-head", (since this was the only part of my body that was protected.) My bike was about to impact her car, and sensing my imminent death, a feeling of deep peace overtook me and I let go of the handlebars; I let go of trying; I let go of the fight. However, there wasn't a 'me' that was choosing this surrender – surrendering just happened.

Very slowly, I started to float upwards and above the entire scene. As I floated up in the air, I remember smiling and laughing with utter relief as I thought to myself: "This is great – I don't have to worry any more about bills, about my overdraft or about finishing with my boyfriend!"

I saw people down below me, but they were transparent. Objects were just paper-thin façades. I started to realise that nothing had any solidity or reality – it was all a dream. Nothing was real or had any importance and there was no such thing as 'time', because all of this was happening outside of time.

And as I rose higher, I felt such an intensity of lovingness around me. It felt as though I were being tenderly embraced by a deeply benign presence. I felt so safe and loved and happy, yet there was no-one to be seen.

Then I became aware that I was enveloped in green-ness. There was beautiful green light surrounding everything, like on the stage at a pantomime where the lights have turned to green, except this green was just heavenly and indescribably glorious. It all felt so thrilling and blissful at the same time. The green-ness made me feel like I was in a forest.

Then I noticed all the doors - they seemed to be built into trees. About 6 closed doors encircled me. I was excited about them. I felt sure that behind each door was the most amazingly wonderful experience. I somehow knew that whatever lay beyond the doors was totally safe, colourful and joyful. I was about to open one door, when all at once I was on the ground looking up at a large crowd of shocked people, including the female driver of the car, who was now staring down at me crying and scared, obviously thinking I was dead.

But I wasn't dead, I didn't even have a scratch or a bruise; nor was I in shock. In fact I was able to get myself up and brush myself down. Yet the outward effect of the accident was devastating to look at.

My motor-bike had crashed into the car and I had been literally dragged through the back window of the vehicle at enormous speed, as if I'd been fired from a canon and then out through the windscreen. The car and the motor-bike were completely 'written- off' and there was glass and debris all over the road. No-one could believe that anybody could have survived such an accident, let alone come out of it completely unharmed.

I'm sure that because of the surrendering (by no-one) at the moment of impact, 'presence' had taken me 'out of my body' at the crucial time and I was fully protected, because there was no longer an '*I*' to fight against the flow of events. *Allowing* was the key, yet allowing wasn't a choice made by any-one, it arose spontaneously.

Since then, there has never been any fear of death, also coupled with a knowing that there is no death. And yet, there had been a kind of death that day – the death of the 'me', of any idea of a separate individual. The dream of separation was seen through into the absolute Oneness of All.

Here is another story: In 1982 I married Alan Johnson (the love of my life) and this marriage took me further into Spiritual interests. Alan had been a Transcendental Meditator for fourteen years, and I followed suit. He also studied Japanese Tea Ceremony for 7 years, which is another form of meditation, and I became his 'Hanto' (Tea-ceremony assistant) and we performed special Tea-Ceremonies for anyone who was interested, for friends and for special occasions.

Alan was also very artistic and pursued lots of hobbies, including pottery & paper-making etc. He died in 1990 of a brain tumour and I was completely devastated.

I have included a picture of Alan surrounded by some of his beautiful creations: his pots and Ikebana flower arrangements.

In an attempt to recover from the desperate pain of grief, I deepened my Spiritual Search, and joined a variety of religions, such as Christian Science, which I stayed with for many years, then various schools of Buddhism. However, I never really liked the reliance on rules and dogmas, and the necessity for groups of people worshipping together and I didn't care for 'worship' in any shape or form, whether to Gurus, teachers, or God.

However, I really liked Zen, and especially Taoism since here was something that didn't include rules, dogma or group participation, or dedication to Gurus.

Then I came to the practice of 'Being in the Now'. It seemed such simple truth - if only I could learn to keep it up for long enough! Unfortunately I only seemed to be able to manage it for very short intervals and had to constantly remind myself to do it, although it afforded me great peace. But this is not what is being talked about in this book. What is being spoken of here is 'Being' itself.

Finally, I read books about Nonduality and especially the writings of Tony Parsons. Then one morning something occurred: I woke up in my bed and 'I' wasn't there. I was everything and everywhere but there was no *me* – no location to 'Mandi' – no Mandi. And there was the sense of a greenish-black colour within the place that use to be me and surrounding everything. The world as I had known it seemed to have evaporated and the mirror reflected nothing more than a phantom. 'I' had died – there was simply no 'Mandi' any more. Pouff! She was gone, and I saw she had never existed at all.

However, things still needed to be done and somehow, they got done. For instance, some items were needed from the market. But first, clothes had to be applied to the body. Somehow I got dressed but there was no *I* doing the dressing – clothes were simply being put on, by no-one. Then tea was brewed and breakfast made and eaten, followed by a walk to the market. Acting happening, yet without the *actor*. At the market there were people who knew 'me' and came up to talk to 'me' but the difficult thing was   having to pretend that I was 'in'.

These 'ghost people' looked into my eyes as they were speaking to me as though I was a person, as though someone was home – but nobody was home! Words somehow came out the mouth, but 'I' wasn't speaking them.

Soon after this shift, there followed some time of apparent contraction – like a drifting in and out of 'This', and then seeking dissolved away completely without a 'me' noticing. Of course, there was no 'time after the 'shift' – this was just another subtle dream - there is no time – just a thought *now* of time passing. There is no 'journey' – there is only *this* – just whatever's happening presently.

Now life is simple and ordinary. It is simply whatever is happening filling all space but with no-one there seeing that: just whatever is happening: stroking the dog; pouring a cup of tea; reading a book; walking in the woods etc. –but because no-one's doing any of it, there's such an *aliveness* to it. For example: 'I' use to feel that 'I' was living life, but in fact life is living me – 'I' am being lived through.

"What's Love Got To Do With It?"

Love has everything to do with 'It'. Love *is* 'It'. Tina Turner's song goes: "What's love got to do with it? What's love but a second-hand emotion?"

But Love is not an emotion. Emotions comprise of feelings, created by thought, such as: need, fear, jealousy, yearning, longing, misery, happiness, excitement and so on, but true love has nothing whatsoever to do with these fleeting and constantly changing fluctuations in thought energy.

So, what is the nature of Love? It is unemotional, non-possessive, utterly supportive, truly compassionate yet impersonal. Love is pure; It is whole and complete within it's own nature – it needs nothing and nobody to sustain itself. Love is boundless; limitless; 'without end'. Love is energy, the DNA, the very 'stuff' of Life – it is Life and is Life-*giving* and Life-maintaining, just like the sun. And Love is also the Sun because Love is everything. Love is God, Life and Source. Love is also you and me – but there are no 'you's' and 'me's'; no separate blue or red facets – just the one colourless diamond that appears as many separate colours.

Love is creation – it exists in and of itself and has no need of anybody to uphold it. It is light and luminous yet indestructible and eternal. It is the Source and is always there and never leaves us, because it *is* us. Like the diamond that produces the effect of all those apparently differing colours, it is just Being which produces the effect of an array of different individuals. And as reflecting facets of the one diamond we can of our own selves do nothing.

As it says in the Bible (John Ch.5 v 12): "Of mine own self I can do nothing." And later in John 14. v 10: "It is the Father that dwelleth in me, He doeth the work".

This is really saying that if I think I exist as a separate individual, then I have no power and no real strength. However, as the 'veil' gradually dissolves, and it is seen who 'I' truly am, then there is nothing that cannot be done or known. The veil is woven by 'attachment thoughts' - thoughts that obscure the truth of who I really AM.

I am Love, and *as* such, I am complete, *All*- mighty and all-powerful.

Love is so often misunderstood. Even though we are composed and comprised of it, Love cannot be known because Love is unknowable, intangible, invisible, in*div*isible, limitless, infinite, immortal and All Power and we cannot possibly be separated from it, because we *are* It.

One of the greatest causes of suicide is the feeling of acute loneliness, separation and isolation, resulting in feelings of desolation and desperation. The thoughts consist of not feeling cared about, a lack of affection or cherishing etc. But in truth there *is* no lack of care or love – because Being, *God,* is everything. 'This' is true beneficence.

No 'other' person can give us what we already have. This is why we can rarely find the perfect partner when we are looking for only human and material characteristics.
We have more chance of finding the right partner, whether it's in love or in business, when we see that we already *are*
that which we seek. Everything we are seeking in another, we already have within ourselves. We are the Whole and therefore we encompass every quality of love that we seek in another.
"Divine Love always has met and always will meet every human need" Mary Baker Eddy

What is meant by this, is that actually there are no humans therefore there are no human needs; all there is *is* Divine Love and so that which is sought has already been delivered.

When 'human' cells are observed, they are continuously repairing themselves. The entire nature of Being is self-healing, self-adjusting and self-supporting. The substance of Life is Good, (which is another word for God.) All that is going on is Good and everything is in complete balance. Any appearance of BAD or evil, has no reality, because the foundation of everything *is* pure beneficence – pure Love.

There is no 'I' – there is only 'All'. When things are being *done*, they are being done *by* no-one. If I want a cup of tea and I go and make one – there is in fact no 'me' making a cup of tea – tea is simply *being* made, by no-one; ultimately, the tea is being made by God. (*Being* making tea!)
Remember there is no 'I' - the impression of a 'me' is simply the result of a continuous stream of thoughts that arise in an identifying of 'myself' as the Source. But there is no individual at the source of Being – the Source of all being is God / Life / Love. So God brushes your teeth and washes your hands, takes you shopping and buys your clothes, feeds you and

looks after when you're ill. You think *you* are doing all of that but there is no you. 'You', are *being* done!

When this is clearly recognized, all the seeking falls away and the gratitude that is felt is truly awesome. Sometimes gratitude is felt so deeply it brings a lump to the throat. We are *never* alone and left to fend for ourselves. We are always *all-one* and *be*loved, reflecting love. Love is the 'stuff' we are composed of. There is only completeness, whatever the outward appearance. There isn't a 'me' that is located in the body - 'I am ' everywhere – everyone and everything – 'I' fill all space and I also *am* all space. Lack does not exist in nature.

The mind, or rather our thoughts, are obsessed with lack – in particular *lack* of money or *lack* of the right partner – or *lack* of ease – so then we experience *dis*-ease. The more our thoughts concentrate on lack, in this dream we're living, the more lack appears in our experience.

But when we are intimate with Being, there is the seeing of continual abundance, because Being both fills and *is* All Space. There is no difference between the basic substance of a chair, a concrete floor, chocolate, or a human etc. – it's all energy –'spiritual substance.' All is *God/Being/ Presence* – etc. 'We are made in His image and likeness'.

Being is both full and empty at the same time.

'Full', because 'I am' everyone and everything.

But also 'empty' of a person, a 'me ' an identity or centre. Nobody's home.

There is no-thing outside of 'I' and therefore no attachment to anyone or anything because 'I *am*' everyone and everything.

Just thoughts arising – one after another after another. Thoughts are simply energy, or *Being,* vocalizing itself.

Thoughts are continuous because *Life* is continuous. Thoughts are no more than fluctuating frequencies of energy that we *hear.* For this reason, thoughts can never be taken seriously because they are subject to constant change – just like the weather. If the weather appears cold and wet, thoughts may automatically become 'miserable' – alternatively, if it is a warm, bright sunny day, thoughts may become positive and uplifting. There is no deep foundation to them – and 'you' are not creating them; they endlessly generate themselves. We become mesmerised into thinking that our thoughts are *us*, that 'I' am my thoughts and also that which I *think.* Yet there is no solidity to 'me' – 'I' am a complete myth. 'I' am just another thought arising in Presence. There is no me and no you.

The Bible says: 'Be still and wait on God'.

In that short sentence, so much is being said. The 'stillness' is the still, immovable 'I am' presence or *Being* – that which is our true habitation.

It is never 'shaken' no matter what is apparently 'stirred'. In the midst of a mad, noisy, rushing crowd, Being is utterly still and unmoved. BEING *is* God and God is everything – it is All in All. There is no place or space where God isn't. Mary Baker Eddy, founder of Christian Science, describes it this way, in her book: 'Science & Health, with key to the scriptures;'

The Scientific Statement of Being

"There is no life, truth, intelligence nor substance in matter.

All is infinite Mind and it's infinite manifestation,

For God is All in All.

Spirit is immortal Truth; matter is mortal error.

Spirit is the real and eternal; matter is the unreal and

temporal. Spirit is God and man is his image and likeness

Therefore man is not material - 'He' is spiritual"

We are all connected – all 'It' - we just don't see it. There is no 'out there' or 'in here'. Everything in the Universe is connected – is one Energy field –Life –God. 'You,' are also the chair you are sitting on, and the floor, the wall, these words, the dog or cat, etc. are all comprised of this same apparently empty yet *energetic* substance. It's all the same thing, including thoughts.

'I' am the content and presence of everything – the height and depth and length and breadth and *Breath,* of everything. There is nothing outside of Me. I am 'It', including 'you', thoughts, and whatever is 'Being' done at the moment. I am everything and all. I am the sun that rises and sets – I am the moon that waxes and wanes – I am 'you' reading this – 'I' am reading *My*-self.

'You' are being thought – 'you' are not thinking. Every time there are 'me' thoughts, you are being 'thought up'. You are not doing anything, you are being done. Everything is Being, *Being* itself.

All action is 'Being' *acting*. For example, there is no 'you' to choose to move a finger, a hand, an arm or a leg. They may move at any moment. You may have noticed that a leg crosses over it's other leg, or a head rest on a hand, without any decision from you. Why did it move at that precise moment and not 2 seconds earlier? Because 'you' are not choosing this – there is no 'you' to decide or choose anything – things just happen and arise spontaneously - and you thought *you* were dong it!

Once again, Mary Baker Eddy, founder of Christian Science, puts this so well:

"God, Being, is the Source of all movement and there is nothing which can retard or inhibit it's perpetual harmonious action". Mary Baker Eddy

As the philosopher and author James Arthur Ray notes: "If you ask a Quantum Physicist : 'What created the world – he would say: 'Energy'. So you say: 'Describe energy'. He'd say: "It can never be created or destroyed. Always was and

31

always has been everything that ever existed and always exists. It's moving into form, through form and out of form".

But then if you ask a Theologian: 'What is God?' He'd say: "It can never be created or destroyed. Always was and always has been everything that ever existed and always exists. It's moving into form, through form and out of form".

So the Physicist would describe 'THIS' as '*Energy*' – the Theologian would use: '*God*' . It's the same description, just different terminology. So if you think you are a body, think again. 'You' are a localized concentration of energy in a more Universal field of energy.

However, this is all 'food' for the mind – for the intellect, and means nothing in terms of true seeing - the seeing through and beyond people and objects by no-one. 'Glimpses' 'peak experiences' and 'energetic shifts' can arise, followed by much harking back to these experiences, which just creates more seeking and less chance of *Being* being seen at all.   Peak experiences and glimpses do not even come close to the absolute simplicity of *This*, which is only that which is going on right now. Just whatsoever is happening now is all there is, whether it be excitement, tranquillity, depression, anger, joy; or no particular feeling. Perhaps huge concentration on something, or just watching TV, reading a book, drinking tea -

just whatever is the case, *presently.* This pure presence is home.

This 'whatever is happening now by 'no-one', *is* 'It' and it is that which fills all space. It is all there is and all that is going on presently.

There is only lightness and wholeness and abundance and it is impossible to feel lack of any kind amidst all that is full, limitless and brimming over with Love, with Life.

The gratitude for this, is constant and beyond words. Love fills all space. There could never be loneliness, or alone-ness or ever a time when Love was not present.

There is no Time – no past, no future – just This, right here – there *is* only 'here' because there is no 'there'. You cannot be outside of This. Everything you can see is all within your 'I am-ness'- it is an extension of 'you' and your awareness. Even that statement is a contradiction as there is no 'you' to *be* 'aware'. This is why it's all so impossible to write about, yet that's why there are so many words used to attempt to describe the indescribable- ness of it all!

All that arises is magical and mysterious, in that it appears from out of nothing and nowhere and is always a complete surprise. For instance: even though I've walked my dog

Howard, in the park a hundred times before, it's really only the thought *now* that I've walked him a hundred times before – in Truth, I am walking him now for the very first time and, when watching him running so excitedly to the park, it's so clear that he's never been there before, either!

There is a famous Zen saying which sums it up nicely: 'You can never put your hand in the same river twice'. Meaning that you could arrive at the same spot by the river, every day, at exactly the same time, but the water is always different – always fresh and new. This is a truth which has been proved through Quantum Physics, demonstrating that cells, atoms and quarks, etc. are dying every second and new ones are being created and replacing the old ones continually. Everything appears from out of no-thing and is continually new and then disappears into no-thing, arising like bubbles and bursting again.

There are no people, just thoughts. Thoughts such as 'Me' – 'mine' – 'hers' – 'his'. As soon as we look at those all-too-familiar terms we can immediately see how the mind separates, categorises and judges everything. Yet these thoughts can sound so loud inside the head, but a thought can never be found. (In Quantum Physical terms, thoughts are merely fluctuating frequencies of energy.)

'I', am just an idea; a thought arising in Being, in THIS. That is why the mind will never grasp THIS, because it *is* the mind which thinks it is reading and processing these words, whereas Presence is seeing itself in the spaces between the words.

So how will all this help? What's the point in even reading these words? The answer lies once again in those Biblical words: "Where two or three are gathered in my name, there I am among you".

When 'you' are reading words - words that arise from Presence, a relationship is established in which we are joined in the *resonation* of Being, of God. Since these aren't 'my' words, and there is no 'you' reading them, (only Presence reading *Itself*) the seeing of This can happen through Being resonating with what is being heard on a deeper level than thought.

Money makes the world go round

What is the nature of money? Money is love. It is divine provision; abundant supply; it is Oneness and cannot be divisible from it. It is the same energetic substance as everything else in the appearance. 'You' can not possibly have any lack of 'money' because it is not outside yourself and so you cannot be separate from it. Love is all and contains all. Money is love made manifest: as gratitude, exchange, payment, winnings, inheritance and gifts etc. – in other words it is all love. And love is Source and is magnetic and just attracts more love. It is only when we become mesmerised by a false belief in the idea of *shortage* or *absence* that 'lack' appears to be the case. Yet this can never be the case, because the belief of anything *outside* of ourselves is a dream. There is no 'outside'; no matter how hard we try we just cannot get outside of Being, of love. And Money is love – it is not outside of us and can never be lacking.

There is no lack of love in Being, there is only fullness. This is seen in nature all the time: in the countless leaves on bushes and trees; blades of grass; people; electrons and photons etc. Love fills all space and *is* also the space it fills.

Love or one of it's countless other names – in this case 'money', cannot be pinned down. It doesn't come through hard work and effort; it can't be owned, bought, sold, stolen or even given away – because money is not material, it just looks that way. But we already know that all appearances are illusory and have no solid, individual or separate basis, so we can perhaps see that pieces of money are comprised of the same concentrated energetic substance as humans, furniture, nature and the Cosmos. This substance is beyond description and yet everything is comprised of it including the space in-between it. *'I'* include all things: I am the chair, the human, the grass and the trees and I am also money because I am love. We cannot lack that which we *are.*

The mind-made attitude to money is that it is something separate from 'me' and is 'man-made' so therefore only *man* could *make it* and usually through considerable work and effort .This is always the thinking when we imagine ourselves to be separate.

I sometimes teach singing, and one of the things I'd do in a bid to attract more pupils , was to drive to many different areas looking for shops who would display my singing advert cards in their windows. I would spend lots of time, money and effort doing this, to little avail. Hardly anyone would ring to book lessons.

Now things are different, since there is no *I* to 'do' anything. Sometimes a thought arises about singing lessons, often accompanied by sitting and staring blankly into space. Then sooner or later the phone rings and someone books a lesson! This happen so often and it's nothing to with a 'me'. It was only when the sense of an 'I' had evaporated, that things could arise spontaneously and effortlessly as and when required. Pure, effortless Being with no-*one* in the way.

'What's it all about, Alfie?'

What is the nature of seeking? The nature of seeking is Love. Love both fuels and maintains the search for *Itself*. However, the mind takes the seeker completely in the wrong direction and as far away from itself as is possible to go. Love is light – yet the mind searches in all the darkest places.

Recreational drug users; criminals; alcoholics, workaholics or sexaholics, are all examples of those who feel such an overwhelming feeling of separateness from the Whole, they are on a desperate search for 'home'. Even the term 'holic' – like the word: 'holistic,' means 'whole'. Looking for the 'whole' in either drugs, crime, sex, work or alcohol – looking for something on the *outside* , except there is no *outside;* yet in not seeing 'this', lies the fruitless nature of the search.

A pop music journalist who was interviewed on Television recently, was being asked about a young, newly –famous, female pop star, who was addicted to Heroin.

The journalist was asked specifically about why that particular drug was so popular with young musicians, especially in the pop world.

He answered: "Heroin feels like a big hug from your mother." Then he went on to say that young people who become famous overnight, in the rapidly changing, super-charged, fickle and superficial world of pop, are desperate to feel a sense of safety in an unsafe, unstable world and that's why drugs are used, especially Heroin .

Ecstasy, is another type of drug that promotes strong feelings of 'lovingness' and reaching out and being tactile. Other drugs, such as alcohol, leads to forgetfulness as does Marijuana, but in a more 'chilled out', spacey way that temporarily avoids emotional pain and mental 'noise'. Cocaine, on the other hand, like Amphetamines, causes 'speediness' – which is just another attempt to avoid the 'way things are'. In fact all recreational drugs have these similar 'escapist' effects.   Also, for people who are workaholics, sexaholics or TV addicts etc , there is the similarity in wanting to 'lose oneself' in the activity.

The ultimate aim of all of these habits and addictions is to loose 'the self' and at last find peace, even very temporarily, and a desperate need to 'come home'.

'Spiritual' seeking is no different – it may be less dangerous, but no less blind, and the aim is exactly the same – to find 'home'. And 'blind', because meditation; guru-devotion; angelic channelling; UFO communication; crop circles and all the rest, are still the search for either something to *happen*; or for someone outside of myself to help me towards enlightenment or for some Alien from another world or 'spiritual dimension' to communicate with me. Then I would feel 'special' and superior to other mere mortals who have not been so blessed. Being 'spiritual' not only means that I get to feel special – but other people get to *see* me being special!

But for those for whom Being is all there is , life couldn't go on more *un*noticeably or be more ordinary - simply whatever is arising presently: lying in the bath listening to the radio – feeding the dog - making the tea – peeling the potatoes etc.

Nobody else knows what you're doing – they can't see you in your house – nobody cares and everyone else is doing the same thing! No-*body's* doing anything anyway! All there is *is* This - just Oneness peeling the potatoes.

And so the search for what we already are continues. No-one can do anything about stopping the search because there are no people. However, it can occur that if this message gets truly heard, beyond the superficial level of thought, if there's a resonance with *Being*, then it could be that the mind finally gives up and there's an end to the search.

This also may never happen; or it could just suddenly happen for someone who's never even heard of Nonduality. One thing's for certain however: getting desperate or depressed about it just keeps the search going – it *fuels* the search. However if it is seeking which is presently arising, then that's what IS. Mind is always moving, longing to be anywhere but *here* and *now*, totally unstable and unreliable . *Being*, is still as a calm lake and stable as a rock, and can be utterly depended on.

Just because it's empty it doesn't mean
we have to fill it.

I AM

I AM the light that wakes up the morning sky

And the dark that closes it down at night

I AM the kite that flies on a windy day

And also the wind that causes the play

I AM the boy that's running with all his might,

Holding the cord that's guiding the flight

I AM all that lives and moves and breathes

People   animals   oceans   trees

I AM every human that's ever been known

And beyond the body, flesh and bone

I AM every thought that shocks or surprises

And every emotion that arises

I AM love and anger, joy and fear,

Passion and peace, or a fallen tear.

I AM beyond description or spoken word

And beyond seeing and cannot be heard

I AM totally invisible yet everything seen

Neither past nor future but have always BEEN

'I can see clearly now'

Sometimes, when people begin attending Nonduality meetings or reading about Nonduality, they can start to feel 'detached' from life, and this may lead them to assume they've found the 'answer' they were searching for – they've finally 'got it' - they can see it all clearly now. Life is different now – they are detached. But being detached is not what *This* is all about and misunderstanding arises through mis-reading or mis-hearing what is actually being pointed to. The mind is trying to grasp the un-graspable - Being can never be understood. Understanding is just another thought – it's more seeking.

Some people say things like: 'Now that I'm 'into' nonduality I feel quite detached from life and I just can't talk to my friends the way I use to – I'm no longer interested in their trivial conversation and I don't know how to talk to my boyfriend because he just doesn't *get* this." But this is just a trap set by thought, to keep alive the seeking (and never finding) and also to enjoy a little superiority, which the mind just loves, because it prolongs the separation. Yet ironically, in projecting itself in a superior manner, the mind is upholding it's belief in separation, resulting in such thoughts as: '*I'm* more spiritual than *you*! I am profound, whereas you are superficial and shallow and on a much lower 'level' to me' etc.

In pure *Being,* there is no-one, so nothing is personal and the nature of 'It' is non-attachment. This is completely different from 'being detached', which is totally mind-made and contrived since there's no-*one* who can *be* detached.

Non-attachment is pure, real, alive, innocent and effortless. Detachment is tainted (because it is unnatural) false, dead and joyless. The mind is very good at fooling a person into assuming they're enlightened by creating an attitude of detachment, which can lead to feelings of 'being lost in a desert'. This is a 'state', and it is frequently described by spiritual teachers as a 'necessary stage in the journey towards enlightenment'. This is completely misguided and has nothing whatsoever to do the seeing of *Being* by no-one – nothing whatsoever to do with *This.* Just THIS that is arising presently and filling all space right here this moment. How can there possibly be 'stages' to reach that which is this present '*now*'? It's an absurd notion.

The following little story may perhaps point to what is being expressed here – about the difference between *detachment* , (which is mind-made) and *non-attachment*, which is the natural expression of Being.

(Bear in mind that this little story is only a 'memory' which is a thought arising presently, about an apparent past.) :

'When my husband was alive, he was an excellent potter and for some of the years we were together, we were interested in Buddhism and meditation. One day, Alan made me a gift of a beautiful Buddha which he had made, and I treasured it. Some years after he died, I brought the Buddha to Hebden Bridge, where I live now and I placed it in my tiny garden and it looked great. (It was also the last remaining piece of his pottery that I owned).

One morning I went into the garden and discovered that my precious Buddha had been decapitated and his hollow head impaled on the railing spike at the side of my garden. It sounds quite comical, but actually it looked quite sinister and cruel.

In response to this, many passionate feelings arose, such as: shock; anger; disappointment; sorrow; yet those feelings were raw and alive. When there was shock, the 'shock-ness' totally filled all space – and that's all there was – there wasn't a millimetre of space where there wasn't any shock – shock was all there *was* – shock was IT!

Next, emerged the red heat of anger like a Volcano erupting taking up all space. Anger was all there was – anger was IT!

These raw, fully alive, electric feelings were EVERYTHING - all that was going on, yet there was no-one 'in' to feel them –nobody home - feelings without a 'feeler'. Nothing was suppressed – not anger, sorrow, tears, etc. – because there was no-one to suppress them – no-one to deny them. The feelings were un-tampered with, un-interfered with, uninterrupted . In this natural unfoldment, the feelings combust and then burn out within minutes –seconds – just like 'spontaneous combustion' – a sudden eruption with absolutely nothing remaining. A burst bubble.

Had there been an 'I' - the situation would've been taken very personally. When there's still someone 'in', when the mind is playing the game of detachment, there is an unnatural suppression of the feelings. The game is: 'I'm detached – nothing bothers me'. But this is just a 'mind-made' state – a 'pretender to the throne' – an impostor. There is still someone there who believes they are a person who can choose to be detached and who therefore lives in a dead, joyless world created by thought. People who act detached are in fact the biggest seekers of all because they still believe there is something to be detached *from!*

This story of the 'Decapitated Buddha' happened, but there was no-one it happened to yet it's quite entertaining to think that it might've been a reflection of what happened to 'Mandi' – 'she' apparently became headless! But that's just a story too. There isn't anything that isn't a story.

Going back for a moment, to the matter of acting detached: it takes an enormous amount of effort (and misery) trying to maintain it. For instance, a 'special' persona must be created, which of course includes various lifestyle changes such as stopping smoking, drinking, swearing or having sex etc. Getting rid of the television and becoming vegan perhaps; wearing fair-trade hand-dyed non-bleached clothes, at all times. Also, one would have to *appear* enlightened which would include both looking *and* sounding tranquil; never saying much at all, thus giving an air of innate wisdom. And then comes the question of whether to smile or not to smile?

Smiling *sparingly gives* the impression that you know something that no-body else does; *or,* you could grin incessantly like a Cheshire cat; this gives the impression that a state of permanent bliss has been achieved - a prize that only *you* have won, but others will probably never attain. And finally - whatever you do - you MUSTN'T *WATCH TELEVISION!*

Oh to be a Guru, now that April's here!'

TV or not TV?

That, is the question,

since being a Guru is now my profession.

My life must reflect transcendental expression,

now that enlightenment is in *my* possession

So I'll have to watch 'X-factor' at my discretion,

and lose Coronation Street in the recession

And no longer watch films with sex or aggression.

Oh no - it's all starting to feel like suppression,

but I think I'm learning a valuable lesson

'Liberation's' not up to my first impression

In fact it's giving me indigestion!

I really don't feel as I *thought* I might

so I'll just see what's on TV tonight.............

Howard's first time on the Beach.

'It's all over now'

When the search is over, all there is, is whatever's going on presently.

The question: 'What is it like for you?' is so often asked, that it may be useful to address, because it's such an erroneous question.

To begin with, there is no me over here, nor you over there. There's no experiencer – no person for whom 'it's like'. 'I' am not liberated or enlightened and no person could ever be, as there are *no* people. Liberation is *all* there is, it is already the case.

However, that doesn't really answer the question that's being asked by the *mind* – and it is only the mind that wants to know what it feels like; so here now is an attempt to describe it, (but it won't satisfy the mind at all!)

What is meant by the phrase: 'It's all over now' is that there is no longer a sense of there being a separate individual searching for something outside of itself in order to feel at peace. That search is 'all over now' and there's no-one there any more to do the searching.

Thoughts of there being something that *I'm* not quite 'getting', seeing or *doing*, are no longer the case and instead, there is only whatever is going on presently.

If whatever's presently going on is: washing socks; frying eggs; sitting reading in the sunshine; crying with gratitude; laughing at something funny; or working out a train timetable, etc. then that is what is filling *ALL* space.

No-one can pretend to see this; there's no practice being prescribed here of 'being mindful' or trying to be 'at one' with what is being done and 'making every act a meditation'. That would mean there would have to be a *person* there attempting to *do* something, in the first place. But when the seeking falls away, and Being is all there is, then there is *only* what is happening in the moment and *nothing else.* Life is just very ordinary because it is filled up entirely by the very ordinary things in life that are going on: feeding the cat; walking the dog; enjoying smelling the flowers etc. it's ordinary-*ness* is all there is.

However it's generally (and mistakenly) assumed that when the 'veil' is 'seen through', then bliss and detachment naturally follow and are experienced by the special One that is the *seer*, combined with a beautiful disposition that permanently exudes tranquillity and peace which can be sensed by everyone. How lovely! How false! The truth is so much more mundane than that.

Firstly, there is no-one *to* 'see' through the veil, also there is no veil. What's more, there would only be 'tranquillity and peace' if that is what was going on *presently*, but if anger were to be there, then anger would fill all space.

Here's a good example from an incident that occurred recently: (And 'recently' is only a thought now about a non-existent past).

I was walking my dog, Howard, down a sloped path in our local park, when suddenly we were almost knocked down from behind, by a very fast skateboarder zooming down the path at enormous speed. He didn't shout out any warning, or slow down and it seemed that either one of us could've been badly injured if we hadn't ducked out the way just in time.

In that moment, fury arose like a huge red vapour filling all space, but that's all there was. Nothing else. No thoughts or feelings – just an angry red mist being itself. No person was there to own, or accept it, or fight against it - it was just there and fully alive in its own vibrant, juicy, angry nature. This rage had momentarily exploded into being from nowhere, and then disappeared just as suddenly back into nowhere, leaving no emotional residue. Exactly because there was no-one there to make it theirs, it left just as suddenly as it came, with no remnant. Next - just peace again.

When the assumption of life as a separate individual is all over, or has been seen beyond, (by no-one) then all that remains is absolute aliveness; and the aliveness includes everything and *is* everything; nothing could possibly be excluded from aliveness. How could it?

Everything and everyone: friends, families, relationships, and all their conversations (whether deep or trivial), also possessions, such as cars, houses and money and attitudes, thoughts and emotions, and peace and war ,
are simply various shades of aliveness. Everything is lived out and experienced fully by no-one. Life is simply lived as it happens, and there's no person there to either be 'attached' or '*de*-tached' to any of it. This aliveness is exactly that – incredibly, astonishingly, awesomely, wonderfully *ALIVE!* It could only be pointed to in words, as the magnificent,

omnipresent, omniscient, vast and boundless eternal presence of Love or God.

Sometimes there are such waves of overwhelming, awesome gratitude for this 'aliveness', that it's beyond words to communicate.

This page has been written in invisible ink.

<u>Your thoughts aren't you</u>

The nature of thinking is joy and pain
Good-bad-good-bad like a run-away train
Separation is always the name of the game
Constantly judging, and fooling the brain
into believing you and thought are the same
But you are *not* your thoughts,
and your thoughts aren't you
Even when they *seem* so convincingly true
And the difference in 'seeing'
and not seeing through
is believing the lie that your thoughts are you
yet you can't stop the thoughts,
because there's no you to do.
And perhaps you feel like your heart is sinking
Under the weight of all this thinking
And maybe you turn to drugs or drinking
when the sense of a *you* is so thoroughly caught
up in every negative thought.

Being is not thought, yet thought is Being

But nobody's there doing the seeing

Thoughts arise and burst like bubbles

Full of fear or joy and troubles

They drift and sail upon the ocean

Energy waves of perpetual motion

Flowing back and forth unseen

Without a *thinker* to intervene

Thoughts alone can not survive

They're just a part of being alive

Yet *Being* is beyond all thought

It is simply *THIS!* And cannot be sought.

Don't go changing

The nature of Being is stillness – constancy –– 'that which abides' - home. It is not subject to change. Being is fullness – completeness and vibrant aliveness and is all in all and therefore it is impossible to be abandoned by Being, by Love.

That which moves and changes is *not* Being – that which is always in constant change and contradiction with itself, is mind. Mind can never grasp Being because it cannot be still – it is always looking for the next event or sensation.

But no-one's doing it - no-*one's* thinking. Thoughts are constantly arising and bursting like bubbles only to be followed by the next 'thought bubble'. But thoughts are all part of Being – but Being is not part of thought – not even thoughts about Being can see Being, yet Being just IS and encompasses ALL. But until Being is seen (by no-one), then the dream continues to create the illusion of people seeing people. And people love to project characteristics on each other.

For example: 'Jane' had always perceived 'Sally' as consistently wise, kind and calm, until one day, when Sally lost her temper and began shouting mean and unkind accusations at Jane. Jane was horrified and from then on, she only remembered that last incident and came to regard Sally entirely differently: now she's a person with a 'dark' angry side which must've been lurking and hiding in the background all the time, and 'kind, wise Sally ' is now forgotten and no longer 'believed in'.

Of course the anger that suddenly erupted in Sally, arose in that moment and for that moment only, but it's too late now for Jane; she hold's Sally forever in this newly negative perception. This is the cruelty and blindness of the false suggestion of separation. But no-one was ever in – nobody was ever home. There are no people to judge or think anything. Thoughts just arise, so the idea of a person with a personality (good or bad) is a mind-made mirage – a dream. 'Sally' was just a character in 'Jane's' dream, moreover, there was no 'Jane' or 'Sally' - just as there is no 'you' or 'me' - only Being. The title of this chapter is 'Don't go changing' but the mind is changing itself all the time and there's no-one to choose to change it or not. Only Being stays constant.

Enjoy this page.

The Nonduality Rap

This is the nonduality ex-mentality cool- reality rap

It's believing in your thinking, when the mind can set a trap;

Those thoughts that have you searching for a way to fill a

gap. But there isn't any gap it's just the mind that keeps you

frightened; into looking to the future for a way to get

enlightened

But no need to look for visions or a 'teacher' *so* inspiring

Or follow just like sheep among the 'spiritual admiring'

You'll never find a teacher who can offer a suggestion

To the desperate, grasping mind that wants an answer to its

question.

There's no-one even out there or in here to *do* the seeking

And Being isn't found in the most eloquent of speaking

There isn't any method or a magical technique

And beware of anyone who says they'll give you what you

seek . But if there's recognition that there is no me and you,

You don't have to go to India to find your own Guru

This 'I AM' presence, so transparent and so clear

is just whatever's happening - it's screaming LOUD AND

CLEAR! It's only what's occurring right now –just THIS- right

HERE!

The Music is in the space

'Non-duality-North'

Non-duality-North is an excellent example of the power of Being and choicelessness. This is the story and it is only a story:

I used to travel to various places, always 'down South', (as termed in the North of England) to visit a variety of Spiritual workshops, Meditation courses, teachers of Buddhist this and that, and then finally communicators of Nonduality. I found it expensive and tiresome to have to constantly travel to these meetings and events but mostly I wondered why 'Spiritual Upliftment' only seemed to happen in the South or South-West of England, and never *here*, where I lived in the North! I also came across others in my part of the country, who felt the same. The 'Northerners' felt that their Spiritual needs were not being catered for!

In England however, there is a long-standing joke between Northerners' & Southerners that there is an imaginary line that separates North and South, called the 'North-South divide!'

Although this is spoken of in fun, it is quite apparent that many Southerners take it very seriously and can be extremely apprehensive of coming to the North of England!

To the majority of them, 'Up North' is an unknown, unexplored territory – probably very cold and rainy most of the time, with no 'Café Lattes' in site, and occupied by natives speaking in a thick, Northern dialect, impossible to understand!

With this in mind, I gently approached a well-known speaker on Nonduality in London, Roger Linden, and invited him to come and visit us here, in Hebden Bridge, Yorkshire, in the heart of the North. It was to his credit that he agreed to come and be the first of his kind to visit Yorkshire and speak about Nonduality. The name: 'Non-Duality-North' was coined as a fun name, as Nonduality obviously cannot be 'split up' into regions, or anything else, but it was chosen for practical reasons: to let everyone know far and wide that these meetings had now become available in Yorkshire. Then the first meeting was arranged and 90 people attended and when Tony Parsons visited us, 165 attended, and so 'Non-Duality-North' began, and has been up and running and expanding, ever since. Roger was the pioneer to whom we were very grateful, because then other Nonduality teachers agreed to come too, and despite all their worries and fears about the North, they actually enjoyed themselves and now come and visit us regularly!

Yet the motivation to create 'NDN' was not a human move. There was no 'I' doing anything, although it appears that 'Mandi' instigated it. Oneness was always the originator. There was absolutely no *one* doing anything – it simply got done and it was effortless. Oneness was simply pushing itself to expand it's consciousness of itself further afield,. 'Being' disguised as people, came to listen to' itself' being expressed – no separate individual caused that to happen - there are no 'individuals'. There was no sense at all of a 'chooser' with a 'project in mind', motivated by a personal *mission* to start something. No person started anything. NDN didn't exist – then suddenly, magically –it did! It arose from nowhere; meetings occurred complete with 'people' – or 'Being' *peopling.*

Of course nothing happened at all – no-*thing* has been created: a meeting happens – then Hey Presto! – 'Non-Duality-North' appears – but when the meetings are over – there is no 'Non-Duality-North' - just nothing and nobody once again, until the next meeting arises – of which there can be no individual's guarantee because there are no individuals. There never was anybody – just Oneness enjoying playful expression of itself. (You can visit Nonduality North by going to our website: www.non-duality-north.com)

Questions

Q. "I have been an avid reader of Advaita / Douglas Harding / Tony Parsons etc. for many years. I feel I have a degree of clarity about all of this, but I am still firmly rooted in the 'self'. Over the years I have become increasingly depressed and de-motivated. I work as an anaesthetist in a busy hospital and just can't be bothered to 'play the game' that is expected of me .'I know that this is just what is happening...and that all there Is Is This, however it is still very much happening to a 'me.' Do you have any crumb of comfort to offer this disturbed but illusory individual?"

"Everything is fine with 'you', just the way it is. No matter how much 'you' think that things are happening to a 'you', it is just not like that.

All that's happening are thoughts arising one after another and things apparently happening one after another but TO NO-ONE. Thoughts arise out of nowhere and then burst like bubbles and return to nowhere. Even the very thought of an 'I' or a 'me' is just another thought arising in consciousness.

Where are you? Can you find yourself? Everything that is happening is happening

PRESENTLY. Depression, frustration, hopelessness, despair or joy, excitement, longing or fears etc. are just emotions and thoughts arising at the time. But no-one's there, they are not happening to anyone; thoughts are merely fluctuating frequencies of energy and are proof of our aliveness.

Everything that you seem to be feeling or going through is just what is there in this moment.   The mind is always wanting to be somewhere other than right here right now. The 'crumb of comfort' is in seeing this - seeing that there's nothing further you have to do. The seeking can end right now. If you've been reading books and going to meetings, then there's nothing else that you will read or hear that will be of any further use to you.   You'll continue hearing the same old message, which is: 'the mind will never see This'. When that is *really* heard, the mind's seeking may come to an end.

Just see that there's nothing you can do. Living life exactly the way it is right now is the whole of 'it.' Recognize the game, but enjoy people and things. If objects seems solid and everyone seems individual and separate, then that's part of the game of illusion too, but you don't have to do anything about that, just let it all be the way it is - there's nothing 'you' can do about it anyway. Because despite you 'seeing' this or not 'seeing' this, the fact remains that anything that appears outside of yourself is illusory and not seeing that is also part of the dream.

So forget about it now and just enjoy whatever is happening presently. Warm bum on chair, breathing's happening, reading's happening. Even if a thought suddenly arises about what you are going to do next, that is still just a thought arising now. It's just the mind that wants 'comforting crumbs' - when it's seen that whatever is presently arising *is* the 'comfort' - then there's no need to search for anything other than what's happening in this moment."

"Everything I've read and heard about Nonduality, resonates deeply....but I feel I am in stuckness.. .it feels like learning to swim or ride a bike...we know its possible but unless we believe IT fully, it won't happen. For me everything comes down to SEPARATION and the belief in it. I can accept intellectually that we are all ONE but feeling or clear seeing is absent. Then the mind comes in and says hang on

here...Tony walks through the park....Nathan cycles down the lane.....Leo gets it from a Beatles record...Mandi finds it waking up in bed one morning ....etc. Are we being led down the garden path here? I know we are not, as IT is the same message the Buddha gave 2,500 years ago: there is 'doing', but no 'doer' thereof . I know there is no you to help no-one here, but this mind/body needs help in clear SEEING."

"Whatever's happening right now, including the feeling that you're not seeing *It* – is also *It*. *It* contains everything, and *is* everything. There is nothing to see except whatever's happening right now – sitting on chair – warm body – reading these words – hearing the birds.

That's It! Just give up worrying about it or wanting it so much (but also accept that *you* can't do that) and go make yourself a nice lunch, because that's *IT* too! When the seeking and grasping falls away, then all there is *is* This i.e - all that is happening *right now*, including thoughts arising. They are not *your* thoughts either – simply thoughts arising from nowhere and disappearing back to nowhere, just like bubbles.

Everything is absolutely fine just the way it is and 'you' are fine the way you are. You may well find that by staying intimate with *This* – with *Being* – that things will gradually fall away and change somewhat. There certainly isn't always a *sudden* energetic shift for everyone, – it can just slowly unfold."

"Ever since I've been 'into' Nonduality (reading the books, going to Talks etc.) life has begun to feel flat and joyless. I don't want to mix with people who don't understand THIS – I don't even know how to talk to my girlfriend, because she just isn't interested in it. Yet I can never go back to the way I was before. Will I always feel like this? "

"Now this is where you have to be very careful. What you are describing here: 'the flat and joyless' – is NOT the *seeing of Being* - it is only the *mind's* intellectual interpretation of *This, and* so often results in feelings of superiority over others who know nothing about Nonduality. But the mind *can't* know Nonduality in any case, since it only sees everything as separate and dual.

I have witnessed this behaviour in seekers again and again at every Nonduality meeting I ever attended- the egotistic, Spiritual one-upmanship that can go on. It is when we become mesmerised by this fake 'know-it-all-attitude that we're least likely to recognize just *Being*, because we are believing that there are *other people out there* in the first place, to *be* better *than*!

There is no-one and nothing outside or separate from Love/Being so you cannot be *more* 'Nondual' than '*somebody else!*' How can 'I' be *better* than 'Myself?'

Being is totally the *opposite* of 'flat and joyless' (although those feelings *could* conceivably arise too, because everything is included in *This.*) However, the true nature of *Being* is *aliveness*- rich, vibrant life with everything included: smells; tastes; sounds; feelings etc.

Every moment is sheer treasure and to cut yourself from apparent other people, is to cut yourself off from yourself - from Life, then that's where feelings of 'flatness' & 'joylessness can originate from.

There really isn't such a thing as 'trivial' or 'meaningful' conversation *or* meaningful. Discussing the price of bacon is just as sacred as talking about nonduality because ultimately the *Being* isn't in the words but includes whatever is happening *presently* and if that happens to be talking about groceries, then that's '*IT*' too. "

"I know its not prescriptive, but which Tony Parson's book were you half way through when you mentioned on your website that you 'awakened' or let's say: 'got a glimpse of how things are seen?' I've read most of Tony's book, Richard Sylvester & lots of others, including Susan Segal's etc , but am still searching and getting tired!"

"Ha! Ha! I have to admit that it always makes me smile when someone asks me the question about which of Tony Parson's Books I was reading when there was an apparent 'awakening'. The question amuses me only because it is the mind that is constantly on the lookout for a formula or a recipe for Liberation, for something to *DO*. But there is nothing that 'you' or the mind can do, and anyway, Liberation is already the case – Liberation is all there is. When the mind finally sees that there is nothing it can do, then all the seeking may drop away.

I could tell you everything I ever did: which meditation I use to practise; the teachers I had faith in; all the books I read, etc. Then you could follow everything I did and it wouldn't be of the slightest help to you, which is why I never actually mentioned the title of the book on my website.

It's exactly like cooking – you could give me the recipe for your special Minestrone soup and I could follow everything you told me to do to the letter, and it still wouldn't taste anything like your soup. It is the searching mind that gets *tired* – eventually it may get so tired that it simply gives up! Then when the mind gives up, *Being* may be seen.

The mind always wants to complicate and separate. Yet the seeing of Being is just the absolute simplicity of whatever is happening RIGHT THIS MOMENT :   the reading of these words – the hearing of music playing in the background – drinking warm coffee – just whatever's going on – just consciousness – just the simple fact of being *alive.* But the mind always wants to be somewhere else – anywhere else other than right here right now. It's always thinking ahead to the next thing that's happening.

There isn't even such a thing as a *'mind'* – which would suggest MY mind or YOUR mind – there are only thoughts arising one after another. We assume an identity with these thoughts and call it 'my mind' – but there is no 'mind'. There is no 'you'. There is only ever just what is happening *presently.*"

"I am sat here in the safe shelter of this nice warm, room.. I've had plenty to eat and drink and I'm comfortable and content and I'm listening to you talking about Nonduality, but I'm thinking about people in other countries who are suffering right this moment.

People who are being tortured, or living in fear of violence close by them; people who are cold, starving, thirsty or dying. What about all their suffering? They know nothing about Nonduality – their world is very real to them. How do you answer this?"

"I am delighted you have asked this question, because it always gets asked sooner or later!

The point is there *are* no people and there is nothing outside of *This* – right here, right now. You may well be sat here thinking about starving people in India, or tortured people in other countries, but the fact is that these thoughts are simply arising *now.* Where *is* India and all the starving people now? Can you actually see, hear, touch or smell them? The very idea of suffering *is* only an idea - a thought of suffering or a suffering thought.

Also when we watch the television and see apparent people crawling in pain or begging for food, all that is actually happening is the TV is showing moving images - phantoms.

There's no reality to these images. If you were to suddenly smash through the screen, there would be no more images.

The dream you live in that witnesses these images, is *only* a dream and there is not even a 'you' who is dreaming it – 'you' are simply being lived through.

I knew a woman who was obsessed with watching the news every time it was on the TV. She felt she *had* to watch it – that it was her duty, or else she would feel guilty about all the supposedly dreadful things going on. But this constant vigil of the news left her feeling that the world was a dreadful, violent, fearful place. As a result of this belief, she seemed to attract bad and fearful events in her own life – in her own 'dream'.

But even the 'woman I knew' was only a thought arising here. There was no woman – no other person outside of myself because 'she' that was also part of 'my' dream.

The truth is that suffering does not exist except in thought, in belief in separation. There can be no suffering in Oneness, in Being, in Wholeness. There can be no Oneness and separation at the same time. Oneness means One-ness and not *two*-ness. Therefore if right now, there is only the consciousness of sitting in the *"safe shelter of this nice*

78

warm, room"(as you said earlier) then that is all that is happening. Nothing outside of this moment in this apparent room. No suffering."

"Probably like many others, I understand the non-duality literature intellectually but there has been no 'ego death'. This is despite having been through Buddhism, reading Krishnamurti's teachings for almost 20 years, attending dialogues, and communicating with some non-duality teachers among other things. A couple of years back I read my first Balsekar book and collapsed into a deep depression. It took some time to recover and resulted in a suspension of the search. I was left asking myself why Krishnamurti had urged individuals to transform themselves, when there is no one who can do such a thing? (Tolle seems to make similar suggestions albeit in a more subtle way.) This body/mind, "me", has now reached the age of 50 and in the face of crisis (both parents very ill, especially my father), their home decimated by last year's floods and still not repaired – leaving me frustrated and angry) the pressure to 'inquire' has re-emerged more intensely than ever. It never really ended. I was always a 'fish on a hook' just waiting to be 'reeled in' when the appropriate circumstances emerged. In the face of the death

of a loved one, nothing seems more important than the understanding of non-duality, but there is nothing 'I' can do to to 'get it'. Is it simply a case of 'grace' choicelessly descending or is there a need for each human being to exhaust all other possibilities first through the search?"

The mind is always on the lookout for formulas, methods, solutions to problems or 'things it can do', and all the writers and communicators of Nonduality you have ever read, have probably told you that there is indeed, nothing 'you' can do – because there IS NO YOU!   This is what is meant by 'nothing you can do'. It is our continuously arising thoughts that create a sense of identity – a sensation of the personal', but if you look for yourself endlessly, you will never find yourself.

We are living in a dream, and all the apparent people and things, both happy and sad, are nothing but apparitions – empty appearances which seem very real – that's the mesmerisation. But when these 'situations' arise, strong emotions can accompany them. But what you are looking for is a way out of these emotions, but there is no escape.

People have the idea that once *This* is 'seen', they will be blissfully happy and free of emotions, but it doesn't work like that. Oneness contains everything including whatsoever arises in the moment.

If somebody you love is ill and suffering, then sorrow and tears may arise. Sometimes the emotions that arise can feel even more raw than before there was the seeing, because now there is a real *aliveness* to then. Anything and everything can arise in *This*, but it seems to be experienced so fully that it drops away very quickly. Feelings can be strongly felt, but by no-one – no *feeler.* For instance, sadness could arise, owing perhaps to grief or loss, but then the sorrow is all there is and fills all space at that precise moment – not a person *feeling* the sorrow – JUST sorrow. Then the emotion doesn't last very long since there is nobody there to *attach* themselves to it.

Also, forget nonduality jargon and such terms as 'ego death' or 'grace choicelessly descending'. This *seeing of Being* is so much simpler than all the phrases so often used to describe it. There is no 'mind' and there is no 'ego' – there are simply thoughts arising 'presently.' There aren't some people who have been given 'grace' and others who haven't. There is just THIS MOMENT and whatever's occurring *in* THIS MOMENT. Is there suffering right now for you, in this very moment? Probably not, because whatever problems seem to be happening, they are all mentally created, and are always about a supposed future, or a past.

You may be able to think back to a time of 'deep depression' or forward to a father who may be dying, but right NOW there is only THIS MOMENT – just presently sitting and reading these words – and there's no-thing else going on.

You've also said: "nothing seems more important than the understanding of Nonduality". Nonduality isn't important at all and there can never be any 'understanding' of it – because the mind will never get This. Stop worrying about it all and what will happen will happen and will fill all space whilst it's happening, whether it be sorrow or pain or joy. The *I am* presence - or *Being* or *God,* is the limitless boundless vastness of Oneness and it is what you already *are.* Nobody can teach you to be what you already are and there is nothing to seek."

"I was kind of settling in to: 'all there is, is me being where I am' and : ' all there is IS this "I" thought', but how does

THAT relate to there not being anyone here ? No- one here IN this ?"

"There is no 'I' that is thinking. Just a thought arising in consciousness – in Being. The misconception is that there is a *you* located there in that space in that body. But there is no you, so there cannot be a location to you. The idea of a you is just another thought. That's all.

All thoughts arise out of nowhere and return to nowhere. No-*one* is thinking them – thoughts just happen.

For instance, maybe you are at home typing on the computer when suddenly the thought arises : 'I'd really like fish & chips for lunch.' But why did that thought happen then and where did it come from?
And why at that particular second and not 2 seconds earlier or 3 seconds later? And why fish and chips and not a pizza? Then, perhaps the phone rings and it's a really good friend, and now you're having a great chat with them and swapping news etc. So where is the 'fish & chip' thought now? It's been replaced with new thoughts, but where did the 'fish and chip' thoughts go? Nowhere. Those 'foody' thoughts came from nowhere, went back to nowhere and

no-one ever thought them in the first place. There are no people and there are no *thinkers* there are simply continuous thoughts flowing like a river - just streams of consciousness."

"What about longing? I haven't had a loving relationship for a long time now and my longing for closeness and companionship and someone to love and Be loved BY, gets in the way of everything. I wouldn't describe myself as desperate or 'needy' – just lonely and a bit weary of it all, and empty. How does nonduality fit in with this?"

"Right now, in this very moment, where are 'you?' The sensors in your fingertips may tell you that you that everything you touch is solid, yet you are not in either your fingertips *or* your body. Can you photograph you? You may think you can, but in reality there would only be a flat lifeless image. Can you record yourself? You may think you can, but there would only be the sounds of words. Are you in the words? Of course not! You cannot find your -self, because all there is, *is* Being. Being is everything and no-thing; – no-thing and *ALL*. There is only ONE-NESS – never TWO-NESS.

Therefore there is no 'you' to *be* either loved or unloved. When this is seen, it is discovered that 'one' is never alone – because there only ever is ONE.

It is always the mind that separates everything and sees 'people' as separate, isolated, individuals. In fact you could never be closer to love because you *are* love and *being* loved, therefore love is never absent and could never abandon 'you'.

Perhaps if you're observing couples, walking hand in hand, and you are seemingly on your own, it could result in your feeling separate and uncherished; but that is only the dream – the dream of lack or incompleteness – the dreaming of something outside of 'you'. But love is all there is, and so it is impossible to ever be without love. This simple truth is seen beyond the mind - in *Being.*

The couple you observed are part of you – if they weren't part of you, 'you' wouldn't be seeing them. If thoughts arise of separation, longing or loneliness, maybe take a moment or two to rest back in the silent comfort of Wholeness, of Being. (This is NOT a practice or a method, because there is no *you* who can choose to do this, but it could arise). Just don't invest time in thoughts of loneliness or lack, because there is no truth in them.

It's just a ridiculous, miserable game that the mind enjoys playing. There are no 'singles' – just ONENESS."

"I fully accept that even before the mind, we are present and aware. This is an undoubtable fact and needs no confirmation, however, can IT be so simple?
Also, I still ask myself: ' why should I discover this wonderful TRUTH while everybody else is walking round (apparently) happy in their separation and would consider THIS as utter nonsense?'
And finally, why does it resonate so much? I sometimes wish IT didn't so that I would not have these doubts about IT......Help!"

"Let's just start with your first sentence: *'I fully accept that even before the mind we are present and aware....'*

Firstly, there's nobody there to accept anything- there's no *chooser.*
Secondly, there is no mind - there are simply thoughts arising presently.

Thirdly, there are no separate individuals to form a 'we'.

Fourthly, all there is *is* Presence or Being - no-body can *be* 'present and aware'.

Fifthly and finally, all that's going on is whatever's is arising presently, so yes - it is that simple. It's only the mind that complicates, through it's need to categorise, separate and *name* everything.

As to your second question: *"Why should I discover this wonderful TRUTH while everybody else is walking round (apparently) happy in their separation and would consider THIS as utter nonsense?"*

There is no need whatsoever for you to 'discover this wonderful truth' - you can't do anything about it anyway! If it begins to be seen, then that's what will happen – if not, then it won't, and it absolutely doesn't matter at all anyway.

As for: *'everybody else is walking round (apparently) happy in their separation'* There are no 'other people'; that belief is just part of the dream . However, these 'dream people may or may not be happy. Most likely they are happy or unhappy depending on whether or not things are going well for them!   That's the nature of attachment and the belief in separation.

And yes, mind always : *'considers THIS as utter nonsense'* as you said, because it's completely beyond the mind.

You also asked: *'Why does it resonate so much? I sometimes wish IT didn't so that I would not have these doubts about IT".*

When *This* is talked about and shared, and when the words spoken come directly from Presence, it's as though God has entered the room. (Not that God could ever leave!), but suddenly Love becomes illuminated – revealed; and then boundaries - the sense of 'my-self' - start to break down and dissolve and then all that remains is Oneness, and there is a resonance experienced - not by a person, but on the level of *Being.*

Finally, you mentioned having *'these doubts about IT".* It's only a thought that could possibly have any doubts about *This.* On the level of *Being,* everything is seen and known.

Even though ultimate reality is oneness and we see lots of projections over this can we still act justly? Is it still ok to campaign for the rights of abused others whist trying to not get so upset by the things we see? I feel a desperate need to campaign against a certain man who is being cruel to dogs.

Everything is included in *This*. There isn't anything that's 'allowed' or not 'allowed'. Who is there to allow it or not allow it anyway?

If there is an urge to campaign, then that's what is there – an urge to campaign. Campaigning or not campaigning will happen with or without 'you'. Campaigning is happening by no-one. It may seem like *you* are campaigning, but there is no *you* to choose it or not choose it. Campaigning is simply that which is arising presently.

I cannot help organizing 'Non-Duality-North'. Really I can't - It has never felt like there was an 'I' who started it – Non-Duality-North simply arose. And one day it may simply stop – probably just as suddenly as it started! Many times, there's been the thought to give it up – pack it in – but it just keeps on perpetuating itself despite 'me'. The 'teachers' seem to keep on coming and the meetings continue arising – but it's all just Oneness lovingly and compassionately expressing itself – it has nothing to do with 'Mandi' there is no Mandi to produce the meetings, Oneness does it all. Because BEING is all that there is and we are being lived through – we are not 'doing' the living. One day Non-Duality-North may stop arising – just as it started.

Another example of 'things arising' : I am sitting at my computer typing away when suddenly there is a scream outside my window. I open my door and there's a woman who's fallen on the ice. Then I walked over and helped this woman up to her feet.

Now that story I have just told you is a dream. It was in my dream that there was an apparent woman 'outside' of an apparent 'me' who needed help. But all of that was a happening, arising in consciousness, because there can be no 'outside' of THIS - there is no 'I' who can be outside of presence. Presence comprises all 4 elements of that story: 'me'; the 'woman'; the 'ice' she slipped on, including the slipping.

It is impossible to get outside of *This.* In the same way, let's take a recent campaign about a man being cruel to dogs. Both the man and the dog are the same - Being *being* everything.

Also, whilst continuing to perceive themselves as separate, everyone has their own little 'campaign' going, and each campaign is different. In this particular instance, it is you the questioner who dreamt up the man being cruel to dogs, and still *your* dream, that conjured up all the other people who seemed to have witnessed the same story and passed it on to each other, till the campaign email arrived in your inbox. But the story and all the apparent 'other people' who read the same thing, were still all part of your story.

In just the same way, nobody would know about the old lady who fell outside of my house unless I told them – this, after all, was only *my* dream. There was no old lady.

All there is, IS just what is arising presently – that which is filling all space.
Right now, right this moment, I am typing. Fingers hitting keys; dog is snoring on sofa; soft ticking of clock and occasional noises from the radiator, and creaking of floorboards. All of that is filling all space and there is NOTHING outside of it. No terrible goings on in Iraq – no Iraq. No men being cruel to dogs. No men – no dogs. I can't even see *my* dog – just hear snoring from behind me – just snoring – can't see dog – maybe he'll appear when I turn round – maybe not. Only that which is presently arising.

So, to come back to your actual question, there is no-*one* to 'act justly' for. There *are* no 'abused others' because there are no 'others'. There is simply just what is arising presently. If you see people being abused in the news on TV – try smashing through the TV screen and see if you can see those people. No. There is only you in your room watching shapes of light in a box accompanied by sounds and mixed together with a 'story', to bind up the ingredients to make a 'horror cake'. It could just as easily be a happy and uplifting story that's the binding agent. But it's all just shapes of light in a box with sounds.

"Is it that all is pre-determined and that free will is really an illusion? Thanks for Your words, which are important in my inner path."

"Nothing is 'pre-determined' – who or what would 'pre-determine' it? Also, there is no 'will' – free, or otherwise. There is only *Being or* Presence. Living from Presence is the ultimate freedom. There are no separate individuals to have a 'will' or a life that is separate. Therefore life cannot be 'pre-determined'.

There is also no 'time' - no future or past, nothing that can be *pre* - anything! There is only ever, 'that which is arising presently' and remember that the presence that wrote these words is the same presence that is reading them! 'You', *Being*, are reading yourself!

There are no separate individuals - this is the illusion – there is only Oneness, therefore we cannot *choose* anything. It only appears that way.

The analogy that I use most often is: If you imagine a huge diamond stretching from floor to ceiling, you would see hundreds of different coloured shining facets. If you go close up to a facet to see one of the colours more clearly, you would find it transparent with no separate colour of it's own - just a part of the whole diamond.

'We', are the same. We seem to be many different people. However, if a Quantum Physicist examined a person really closely with an electron microscope, they would be able to see beyond flesh and bone, beyond atoms and particles, into the limitless, vastness of Being.

They would see there was no 'person' there– no 'centre'. Just pure energy. Pure Being. God.

Also, there is no choosing because there are no choosers.

For example: 'You' may decide that you would like to have a glass of water; that is a future thought – but really it is simply a thought arising now . There is no 'you' to choose anything. So how do you know you would actually get your water? The phone may ring and it 's your friend; so now you forget all about the water.

Your thoughts could change at any moment. You may randomly decide instead to get a glass of wine, or a café latte or an orange juice, or a beer - so you may get the water and you may not. In any case, the 'choice' was just an arbitrary thought arising spontaneously.

Nothing can be pre-determined since God /Being or Presence is Love, and love is impersonal. If it was personal, it couldn't be the vastness, limitless freedom that it is. We *are* that love and that impersonal vastness. We are boundless, perfect, pure, harmonious and free.

Finally, you wrote: *"Thanks for Your words, which are important in my inner path"*.

First of all, it was very kind of you to thank me, as long as you remember that there are *no* words that are 'important'. They are just pointers, and very limited! (Also there is no 'I' saying them.)

Secondly, 'you' have no *'inner path'* because:

(1) There is no you

(2) Having a 'path' implies time – and there is no time. There is only This – here – now. Just that which is arising *presently.* Being can be 'seen' RIGHT NOW! No waiting!

No Self - No Suffering

There is no 'Self' to own a feeling

Or emotion that needs healing

Nor a past that needs revealing

Or a person who needs 'toughening'

To cope with 'their' apparent suffering

And guilt can no more plague a heart

In Oneness, where it has no part

There is no Soul to seek and find

Through practices to clear the mind

There is no Self behind the eyes

Yet Joy or fear could still arise

But no-one's 'in' to sympathise!

No self – no suffering – no-*one* seeing

That this *aliveness* HERE, is *Being.*

The Final Word is ... Love

There is no doubt that Nonduality is about: Love. Love is all there is. It is the creative force behind any project and *is* also the project. Love is compassionate and wide-open, limitless, innocent. And anything can arise in Love because it is like the sun, which shines on both 'sinner' and 'saint' and sees them as all one. And Love, again like the Sun, isn't personal and cannot judge or differentiate – it does not decide who receives it's warmth and light and who doesn't - shining is simply happening. There are no separate beings – how can Being be separate? It's like saying the sun is warm sometimes and at not other times –the Sun is also Being , 'Being seen' as: light.

Love is the heart and soul of nonduality – that is what it is all about. Love includes everything and *is* everything that it includes. Even behaviour which is deemed as aggressive or suffering is still Love demonstrating that there's no-one there to suffer, but also that anything can happen because there is no chooser.

If seeking falls away and there is the 'seeing of Being' by no-one, it is recognized that love is all that is going on and the sense of loving-kindness is so strong that the gratitude for this is truly awesome and indescribable.

It is God, Presence, Oneness, and each facet of Oneness is so incredibly beloved and dear to itself, that compassion is all that is left, when there's no longer any sense of the personal. There is no separation – separation is impossible and nonduality is all about that sense of coming home – yet there's no-one *to* come home – home is all there is.

For 'me', before the sense of a separate self dissolved, I felt like 'I' was a separate stream or river; but then that false perception of separateness fell away, and I rejoined the Ocean –which I had never left. Of course I had never ever left it, but for a time there, I thought I had. But a drop of water and the Ocean are all the same thing.

All there is now is whatever is filling all space. Being is filling all space and is the space that it is filling.

And, as was discussed earlier, there is a natural non-attachment which is definitely not, *de*tachment.

Detachment is a completely false, mind-made forgery of *This.* The nature of detachment is cold, 'choosy', judgemental, non-compassionate and unfeeling, uncaring and unkind and makes a mockery of Love – true Being.

Non-attachment is warm, and deeply compassionate and loves *itself* which includes everything in the appearance. There may be preferences: so not everyone or everything is *liked* – but as it is seen, by no-one, that separation is a false appearance, then Love is all that is ever going on. Everything is allowed – Being is Love – Love is Being and there is a natural loving-kindness – an innocence to all this, that can only come from Presence. In the appearance there may arise sudden anger, but when there is only THIS , anger and preferences are totally seen through.

Hostility and angry feelings cannot remain when there's no person there for them to attach *to.* Being is Love. Love is Being. This is the 'Seeing of Being' by no-one.

This is the joy of NO SELF.

THE ENDLESS ....

Thanks a lot for reading this book and I hope you have
enjoyed it. You can let me know, plus, if you have any
questions or comments, or if you would like to purchase
more copies of this book,
or my CD: 'Love *talks*', please visit:
www.mandisolk.com.
Email: mandi@non-duality-north.com
Or, to find out more about 'Nonduality-North', visit:
www.non-duality-north.com

LaVergne, TN USA
28 January 2010
171497LV00003B/124/P